DEAR READERS &

Believe it or not, you can be both reader and viewer! This hybrid media publication full of fascinating insights has some fantastic surprises in store.

What makes this book MORE?

Our publication aims at providing the next generation with the knowledge of the diversity and characteristics of wild mammals native to Europe in the most spectacular way possible. Also, we believe we manage to raise awareness of how important it is to preserve our natural treasures in a global world. At the same time, we are committed to inspiring our readers to love and protect our flora and fauna.

We wish the whole family a lot of fun and quality time together.

The authors and developers

A GUIDE FOR USING AR CONTENT

1. Download the **AR Books LibrARy** app.

arbookslibrary.com/app

Download on the App Store | GET IT ON Google Play

2. Register and log in.

3. Folow the instructions in the app.

4. Book ID:

MAMMALS

HEAD TO THE FOREST!

The forest is home to animals and plants.

The forest is a world of hidden, mysterious diversity. Wild animals choose their homes where they find the right living conditions.

air **sunshine** **climate**

resting and hiding places **fresh water** **food**

IMPORTANT

Animals really need safe places that provide shelter from their natural enemies and harsh weather conditions.

How many animals can live in an area?

Each area has a carrying capacity, consequently, if an animal species population grows too large, there won't be enough food, and the existence of other species can also be threatened.

Game protection

water in the trough

big game feeder, hay, straw

wallows

salt bins

deer and wildlife fence

traps

shrubbery

forest edges

Have you ever heard of wildlife management?

The aim of wildlife management is to maintain the balance of valuable wildlife as well as its conservation. If there is a decline in the wildlife population, game conservation is particularly important.

Tasks of forest and game managers

- habitat protection
- forest maintenance
- removing dead or diseased trees
- filling feeders and waterers
- placing salt bins
- the creation of artificial wallows
- placing baits with vaccines

The fox...

...is the most common carrier of rabies, so vaccine-baits are used for their immunisation.

WILD BOARS

'Pig wellness': wallowing in the mud.

gilt / sow

The sow's canine teeth which have grown big are called hooks.

boar / barrow

The characteristic feature of the wild hog is its tusks.

Piglets have a striped pattern on their backs. When a piglet grows up, the striped pattern disappears. Subsequently, it is called a shoat.

boarlet / piglet

The sow builds a nest from twigs and dry weeds to keep her piglets warm. The sow will breed 4-12 piglets at a time.

Why do wild boars wallow?

- to protect themselves from the heat
- the dried mud on their bodies gives protection from parasites

What do wild boars eat?

worms, insects, earthworms

tubers

mushrooms

acorns and beechnuts

rats, voles

berries and fruits

remains of dead animals

eggs

agricultural crops

Forest tips:

- If you see a striped wild piglet in the woods, never touch it! The sow can be aggressive if it has piglets.
- If you see an adult boar, do not approach and avoid eye contact.

Wild boars...

- are social creatures,
- run fast,
- can change direction quickly,
- swim well,
- have an outstanding sense of smell.

40km/h

Wild boars cause great damage to agriculture.

RED DEER

Majestic inhabitants of woodlands dotted with clearings.

In spring, the red deer doe normally gives birth to a single calf, or sometimes twins. In the event of an attack, does stand on their hind legs and 'box' with their front legs to protect their calves.

Stags can boast with their magnificant branch-bow antlers.

The hind does not wear antlers, and, as for her size, it is much smaller than the stag.

The calf is reddish-brown with yellowish-white spots.

Deer bellowing

Deer bellowing can be heard during the mating season, in autumn. The stags visit the does. If another stag is with the harem, the new arrival will fight its rival. First, they show off their strength by slashing down trees and bushes with their antlers, and then they attack each other. The winner takes the harem.

Fun fact

A deer herd on the move is a majestic sight. The rudle can be made up of even hundreds of deer!

rudle (herd / mob of deer)

What do red deer eat?

grasses

herbaceous plants

buds

acorns

tree barks in winter

The red deer...

- hide away and rest during the day,
- graze in the evening and at night,
- and often wallow to get rid of parasites.

How do deer live?

- Most of the year, hinds live in families with their calves.
- Stags may be alone or form stag herds.
- Solitary stags are usually the old ones.
- For the winter, deer group together to form a 'rudle'.

Did you know?

Deer cause damage to sunflower- and cornfields.

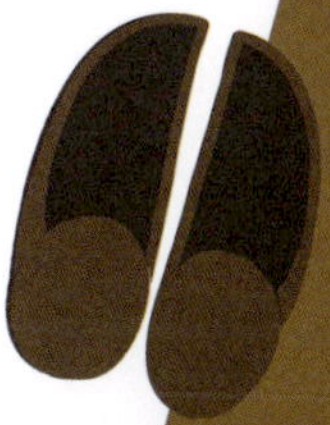

EUROPEAN ROE DEER

Graceful hoofed creatures of woods and groves.

doe

roebuck

Only the roebuck has antlers, which are shed in autumn or early winter, and then they regrow. During the growing period, the antlers are covered with 'velvet'.

kid / fawn

The doe chooses a hidden nook where she usually gives birth to twins. The brownish-coated, white-spotted fawns follow their mother everywhere after 10-12 days.

Did you know?

Roe deer are picky! They look for delicious treats. In autumn, they like to eat seeds and fruit in preparation for winter.

Roe deer cause damage to both agricultural and garden crops.

What do roe deer feed on?

soft and tasty vegetable parts

shoots

buds

shoots and bark of shrubs

Facts about roe deer

- In English they used to just be call roe, but nowadays it is more common to say roe deer.
- In summer, roe does can be solitary or live in small families with their fawns.
- In autumn and winter, they live in larger groups, called rudles / herds.
- Roe deer mark their territory by scent marking.
- The faces of aging roe deer turn grey.

Winter coat	Summer coat
thicker	thinner
longer	shorter
greyish-brown	reddish-brown
with velvet antlers	with full-sized antlers

MOUFLONS

Cautious horned sheep found among the trees.

ram

The rams' heads are beautifully decorated with curved horns. On both sides of their backs, there are saddle-like marks to be seen.

sheep / ewe

Females can also grow horns, only smaller than those of males. They are called horned sheep.

A ewe lamb is a female, which has not yet produced offspring.

lamb

At birth, lambs weigh no more than a kilogram!

Separated from the flock, the sheep usually give birth to one young at a time. The lamb quickly gets to its feet and follows its mother just an hour or two after its birth.

IMPORTANT

The mouflons' horns are also known as helix-shaped horns.

Sheep bleat, rams sometimes growl, but a whistle signals danger.

What do mouflons eat?

grasses · herbaceous plants · shoots · mushrooms · berries · alfalfa · elderberries · pine shoots

Incredible but true

Mouflons never shed their horns, they have them all their lives. On the grooved surface of the horns, growth rings can be seen.

Mouflons are excellent runners and jumpers!

All about mouflons

- Mouflons live in small herds and take care of each other.
- They prefer grazing at dusk or by day; grazing is followed by rumination.
- The herd is led by an older ewe.
- The ewe will only accept her own lamb, she will never care for others'.
- Adult rams form a separate flock.

RED FOXES

Cunning forest creatures on the prowl in gardens.

dog-fox / tod

vixen

After the pups are born, the male fox also takes a role in feeding the fox family.

Female foxes breed once a year. A litter usually consists of 4-8 pups.

pup / kit / cub

The fox cubs are very lively and playful!

The pups are born in grey colour, with eyes closed, ears flattened against the head, and without teeth. The mother fills the den with her own plucked hair for their youngs.

Did you know?

Foxes are good swimmers. They hunt waterfowl and raid their nests.

What do foxes feed on?

Foxes are dangerous chicken thieves!

Golden jackals

The golden jackal - or reed wolf - is neither a fox nor a wolf. This predator, which is bigger than a fox, but smaller than a wolf, spreads rapidly and causes serious damage.

The fox is a cunning and skillful hunter.

Where can fox burrows/earths be found?

- under the ground
- in abandoned burrows of other animals
- in the cavities of sand mines
- under the roots of big trees
- in shrubs
- in haystacks

About foxes

- The fox's good adaptability makes it the world's most widespread land predator.
- The individuals have their own hunting grounds.
- The puppies are raised by their parents together.

GREY WOLVES

Harsh laws in the pack.

he-wolf / dog

In wolf packs, the male also helps nurture and take care of the pups.

The mother wolf produces 4-6 pups once a year. The wolf pups are born deaf and blind.

The mother wolf cares a lot for her pups in the first months.

bitch / she-wolf

The wolf pups love playing with each other!

pup / cub

What do wolves eat?

The wolf is a predator, hunting in packs. They share prey in order of rank. They are not picky at all! From mice to deer, they will prey on any animal, and even scavenge on carrion.

The wolf is the ancestor to the dog.

Wolves are excellent runners and long jumpers!

Where do wolves live?

Wolves live in dens, either by a stream or some other water source. A wolf den can be hidden in rock caves, in the hollows of old trees, under the roots of trees, or in burrows dug into the ground.

den

Wolves live in packs. The leader of the pack is the alpha male, followed in order of rank by the alpha female.

Wolves...

- are social creatures,
- live in packs,
- practise pack solidarity,
- raise and feed their pups together.

Why do wolves howl?

- to strengthen social bonds
- to coordinate hunting
- to mark their territory
- to communicate with each other

BROWN BEARS

Furry behemoths that look very slow.

boar

The bear hibernates in winter, but it wakes up several times. It loses a lot of weight during hibernation, so no wonder he feels extremely hungry when waking up in the spring.

A female bear produces 1-3 cubs. Newborn bear cubs are rather helpless: they are born naked, blind, deaf, and have no sense of smell. When protecting their cubs, female bears can be really aggressive!

sow

cub

Did you know?

Bears do love eating honey. Even bee stings won't stop them from getting it!

Fun fact

Black bears make a soft bed for themselves from dry grass and leaves. They are better swimmers and climbers than their brown counterparts.

What do bears eat?

berries

fruit

grass

mushrooms

roots

carrion

other animals

fish

honey

ants, moths, larvae

The Raccoon...

- is called a washing-bear in many languages, but it is not a bear,
- washes its food before eating it,
- is agile, fast, and excellent at climbing trees,
- is instantly recognisable by its bandit mask.

A brown bear can grow as tall as three metres!

Where do bears live?

Bears hibernate for the winter in their dens. Cubs are born here, protected in the hollows of giant trees or between the roots, in the shelter of trees uprooted by the wind, in rock crevices or caves.

WILD CATS

Clawed little beasts with silky fur.

The female wildcat's fur is yellowish-grey, with a rusty yellow muzzle and yellowish-white chest.

Tom cats are not much bigger than female cats.

Wildcat kittens look very much like those of the domestic cats.

The mother cat has 3-5 kittens at a time, which are born blind, toothless, and with short hair.

What do wild cats eat?

mice

squirrels

birds

Did you know?

Wild cats are rather aggressive, even as kittens. Then, as adults, they can catch a rabbit and even a roe deer!

Where do wild cats live?

Wild cats live in solitude. The mother cat rears its young ones alone. It builds their dens in rock hollows, in tree holes or in burrows abandoned by other animals.

rock hollow

tree hole

Let's compare them!

What are the similarities?

Wild cats and domestic cats look very similar, and they both are dangerous predators.

What are the differences?

The tracks of a wildcat don't show the claws, but those of a domestic cat do!

BADGERS

Voracious masters of underground labyrinths.

Badgers, the omnivorous predators of woodlands, are increasingly frequent guests even in residential areas.

sow

boar

Badgers are restful by day, but they are active at night. They live in clans, i.e. in extended families. The badger setts and their surroundings are kept clean. In cooler habitats, they hibernate in winter.

cub / badger cub

Baby badgers are born either in February or March.

The female badger produces 2-6 cubs at a time. Badgers live together in an extensive sett network.

Badgers love eating. They are voracious, big eaters.

A worldwide sensation!

Secret bunkers 2 metres underground!

What do badgers eat?

Badgers' sett is a networks of dens built over several generations and decades. Some networks consist of up to 50 chambers, with hundreds of metres of tunnels. Plenty of space for sleeping and playing as well!

The wolverine...

- is a bear-like, weasel-like predator,
- hunts solitarily in the Arctic,
- is commonly known as a glutton,
- contrary to its name, is not a big eater,
- saves the rest of its prey for later.

Badgers are very farsighted. They store food for the winter in the badgers' dens.

STEPPE POLECATS

Professional vole hunters in the open fields.

hob

A member of the weasel (Mustalidae) family, the male polecat is much heavier than the female, weighing as much as about 900-1000 grams.

jill

The female polecat is very light, about 600 grams. It produces 3-7 kits per litter, which she rears alone.

kitten / kit

The kits' eyes do not open until they are a month old. Growing polecat kits learn how to hunt from their mothers.

Steppe polecats or ferrets?

Ferrets are popular pets. They are gentler than their aggressive relative, the steppe polecat. Steppe polecats use bird-chirp-like communication, while ferrets communicate with dooking, or squeaking.

The resourceful polecat

The polecat is a predator. It digs for hamsters and voles. It collects and stores all year, so its pantry is always full. In winter, it has a veritable refrigerator!

What do polecats feed on?

voles

hamsters

rats

frogs

eggs

nestlings

Although it is small, it is still aggressive!

Where does the steppe polecat live?

The steppe polecat digs burrows in the river banks or under the roots of trees. In its underground burrow network, it has a separate sleeping chamber, a pantry, and even a toilet of its own above ground!

WARNING!

When escaping or defending themselves, polecats emit unpleasant, foul-smelling secretion from their stink glands.

Did you know?

The steppe polecat is also known as the white polecat (or masked polecat) because some part of its fur is white as if it were covered in flour.

Interesting fact

Just like martens, steppe polecats also pilfer hens. Fie!

EASTERN HEDGEHOGS

Nocturnal wanderers of forests, fields, parks, and gardens.

boar

sow

The backs of hedgehogs are covered with a thick coat, including 7000 sharp, hollow spines, which are constantly replaced. The old ones fall out and new ones grow in their place. Pulling their limbs and head towards their belly, with the help of their strong skin muscles, hedgehogs can roll into a spiky ball to defend themselves in case of danger.

hoglet

Mama hedgehog nurses her 2-7 babies for 6 weeks. The newborn hedgehogs' spines are soft and white. Their skin is pink and their eyes are closed. Their milk teeth emerge on day 21. They first hunt at a few weeks old.

Amazing

The hedgehog can eat a viper since it is immune to snake venom!

Watch out for hedgehogs crossing the road!

What do hedgehogs eat?

worms | earthworm | larvae | snails | insects

The hedgehog is a real wanderer; it can travel several kilometres a night.

The hedgehog...

Hedgehogs are not hogs! It is a misnomer.

- is a solitary nocturnal animal,
- hibernates curled up in a nest,
- can run fast and catch mice and lizards,
- makes a loud hissing sound as it moves,
- 's biggest enemy is the eagle owl.

Where does the hedgehog live?

With its sharp claws, the hedgehog digs a hole for itself to live in. In the winter, it hibernates in a nest made of dead leaves.

At 12-25 cm in size, the desert hedgehog is smaller than any other hedgehogs.

The big gymnure, also known as hairy hedgehog, is a resident of tropical forests. Its characteristic smell resembles sweat or rotting onions.

EUROPEAN HARES

Swift jumping champions in fields and on farmlands.

By day, the European hare - also known as the brown hare - stays in woodland edges or furrows, resting.

Mother hares do not spoil their offspring. During the day, they are left alone, and only in the evening are they nursed.

jack

jill

leveret

The newborns are very independent. At 2-3 weeks old, they can already eat plants.

The mother hare breeds several times a year. 2-5 leverets are born at a time.

Hares'...

...incisors grow continuously, but due to constant chewing, they wear down.

Did you know?

When courting, the buck starts chasing the doe, and then they start 'boxing'.

It can run at up to 70 km/h in zig-zag fashion!

The hare is as fast as lightning.

What do hares eat?

grasses | weeds | clover | grain corps and rapeseed

Interesting fact

To prevent sliding on ice, hares have fine, dense fur on their soles.

What's the difference between hares and rabbits?

The European Rabbit

- lives in a large family
- digs his burrows in the ground
- is smaller in stature
- has shorter hind legs
- has shorter ears
- baby rabbits are born naked
- baby rabbits are born in an underground burrow

The European Hare

- lives a solitary life
- builds a nest for itself
- is larger in stature
- has long hind legs
- has longer ears with black tips
- baby hares are born fully furred
- leverets are born aboveground

RED SQUIRRELS

Playful acrobats of tall trees.

boar

The squirrel is a rodent. The male and female are of the same size. When climbing and jumping, its tail is used for balancing, navigating, and as a blanket at night.

sow

kit / kitten

A baby squirrel is really tiny, just 8-10 centimetres. The female squirrel breeds twice a year, 4-5 offspring. The baby squirrels are naked. Their eyes do not open until they are two months old.

The squirrel is intelligent because...

- it builds several food stores for itself,
- it always returns to its nest at night,
- it makes a reserve nest in case of danger,
- it knows where the weakest part of the nut is and chews it in half there,
- in winter it hardly ever moves to save energy.

What do squirrels feed on?

cones

beech-nuts

bark

nuts

berries

mushrooms

bird eggs

nestlings

insects

Did you know?

Squirrels love playing, jumping from branch to branch. They also like to move to urban parks and gardens. Watch the trees as you walk, perhaps you can spot a few.

Squirrels communicate with squeak-like calls.

Where do squirrels live?

Squirrels build their spherical nests in tree hollows or high branches. They are mostly solitary.

The grey squirrel is much larger, than the red one.

Would you have thought, that the little European souslik is a close relative of the squirrel? Just like the 6 - 8 centimetre-long hazel dormouse and the European fat dormouse!

EUROPEAN HAMSTERS

Tiny gatherers with huge pantries.

Males and females live in burrows in close proximity to each other, yet separate.

buck

The female hamster produces 4-16 offspring several times a year. The pups are born naked and blind.

doe

pup

Hamster pups are really clever; as early as at the age of one month, they are completely independent!

Did you know?

If a hamster is attacked, it stands on its hind legs and snaps its teeth.

rearing hamster

Incredible

A hamster can stockpile up to 15 kilograms of food for the winter!

The grandmaster of gathering

The hamster collects food into his cheek pouch, then with massaging movements, it empties the food into its pantry.

What do hamsters feed on?

greens

grains

fruit

insects

earthworms

snails

Where do hamsters live?

Hamsters live in colonies, in separate, lined underground burrows but close to each other. The burrows have several entrances and exits. The emergency entrance is vertical from ground level into the tunnel. It's like a fast lift. In the event of danger, it can get down in an instant!

underground hideout

Vole relatives

common vole

woodland vole

With a brownish-grey back and a greyish-white belly, the white-legged **common vole** forms radial exits from its central chamber lined with leaves. The **wood mouse** or common mouse has a greyish-brown back and a whitish belly. With its longer hind legs, it runs hopping.

EUROPEAN BEAVERS

Master dam builders of forested wetlands.

male

female

Beavers protect and raise their young with great care.

Beavers find a mate for life and remain faithful to each other.

kit

The beaver kits remain with their parents and siblings until they are about 2 years old.

The parents with the kits live as a small family. One or two beaver kits are born at a time, with fur and eyes open. However, the newborn kits can't swim yet.

Did you know?

The beaver's huge, curved incisors grow continuously, so they chew all the time to wear them down.

What do beavers eat?

herbaceous plants

leaves

bark in winter

Safety first!

Beavers use fallen trees, twigs, and mud to build dams to raise the water level in areas of low flow. This keeps the entrance to their burrows underwater to protect the beaver family from predators.

It is the Canadian beavers, in particular, that build dams.

Where do beavers live?

Beavers live in domed beaver lodges made of twigs, grass, and moss, or dig burrows in the bank, with an underground tunnel system.

Water garden with dam fencing?

The water plants growing in the small pond created by the dam are what they love to eat.

A beaver can weigh up to 40 kilograms!

Beavers cause damage, by chewing around and knocking down trees.

TABLE OF CONTENTS

List of 3D models